APR 1 9 2013

THE SCIENCE OF PHYSICS

THE SCIENCE OF PHYSICS

EDITED BY ANDREA R. FIELD

Britannica®
Educational Publishing
IN ASSOCIATION WITH
ROSEN
EDUCATIONAL SERVICES

Published in 2012 by Britannica Educational Publishing
(a trademark of Encyclopædia Britannica, Inc.)
in association with Rosen Educational Services, LLC
29 East 21st Street, New York, NY 10010.

First Edition

Britannica Educational Publishing
Michael I. Levy: Executive Editor, Encyclopædia Britannica
J.E. Luebering: Director, Core Reference Group, Encyclopædia Britannica
Adam Augustyn: Assistant Manager, Encyclopædia Britannica

Anthony L. Green: Editor, Compton's by Britannica
Michael Anderson: Senior Editor, Compton's by Britannica
Andrea R. Field, Senior Editor, Compton's by Britannica
Sherman Hollar: Associate Editor, Compton's by Britannica

Marilyn L. Barton: Senior Coordinator, Production Control
Steven Bosco: Director, Editorial Technologies
Lisa S. Braucher: Senior Producer and Data Editor
Yvette Charboneau: Senior Copy Editor
Kathy Nakamura: Manager, Media Acquisition

Rosen Educational Services
Heather M. Moore Niver and Shalini Saxena: Editors
Nelson Sá: Art Director
Cindy Reiman: Photography Manager
Karen Huang: Photo Researcher
Brian Garvey: Designer
Matthew Cauli: Cover Design
Introduction by Heather M. Moore Niver

Library of Congress Cataloging-in-Publication Data

The science of physics/edited by Andrea Field.—1st ed.
    p. cm.—(Introduction to physics)
Includes bibliographical references and index.
ISBN 978-1-61530-676-3 (library binding)
1. Physics—Juvenile literature. I. Field, Andrea R.
QC25.S43 2012
530—dc23

                                                                    2011026548

Manufactured in the United States of America

On the cover, page 3: Popularly called Newton's cradle or Newton's pendulum, this device illustrates
principles of motion, energy, and other physical concepts. *Shutterstock.com*

Cover (equation), Shutterstock.com; pp. 15, 20, 34, 42, 48, 54, 55, 68, 69 © www.istockphoto.com/Mauro
Scarone Vezzoso; remaining interior background images Shutterstock.com

CONTENTS

When you wake up in the morning, you probably flick on a light. Maybe you pop some toast in the toaster and then check your e-mail on the computer or check out the latest news on a smartphone. As you will discover in this volume, the science of physics makes all these parts of your morning ritual (and much more) possible.

Because the natural sciences overlap and because the fundamental knowledge of the other natural sciences is based upon physics, it can be a challenge to precisely distinguish physics from the other fields. Essentially, however, physics is concerned with the nature of matter, its basic components, and how all matter and energy in the universe interact, all of which relate to other scientific fields. The two major subdivisions of physics are mechanics (which concerns the motion of objects being acted upon by forces) and statics (the study of matter at rest). Other divisions include optics, acoustics, thermodynamics, and electricity, among many others.

As they try to understand the physical world, physicists attempt to determine invariable laws of nature. One excellent example of such a law is Isaac Newton's law of gravitation, which states that any particle of matter in the universe attracts any other with a force related to their masses and the distance between them.

Perhaps the most essential topic in physics, mechanics unifies all other branches of physics by establishing units of measure that can be applied to all interactions. Some of the most significant work in mechanics came through the work of such scientists as Galileo and Newton. Galileo's experiments with falling objects and Newton's pioneering work in a variety of areas resulted in the discovery of some of the fundamental laws of physics.

Although Newtonian mechanics covered a great deal of ground, scientists were puzzled by a new question after James Clerk Maxwell found that light travels like a wave: what supported the wave? Albert Einstein proposed two revolutionary theories of relativity that helped illuminate some of the flaws in Newton's theories. He provided a new explanation of the behavior of light and showed how certain concepts, such as space, time, and gravity, had to be radically redefined.

Another important concept in physics is that of heat. It was not until the late 18th and early 19th centuries that scientists began to determine that heat was not a substance,

as had been previously believed. Instead, they proposed the kinetic molecular theory, which explains that heat is generated by the motion of the molecules that compose matter. According to this theory, heat can be transmitted and absorbed in any quantity. But in 1900 Max Planck showed that radiant heat energy is actually transferred in precise quantities (like particles). The smallest unit of this energy that cannot be divided is known as a quantum.

Although electricity was the slowest branch of physics to develop, evidence of it in nature is widespread and even ancient people were familiar with aspects of it, such as magnetic stones and lightning. Eventually, electrical activity was found to be the source of light and intimately related to magnetism; all three concepts were unified in Maxwell's theory of electromagnetism in 1873.

The study of light has not been without its controversies. Arguments supporting Newton's view that light rays are streams of particles came up against the ideas of another scientist, Christiaan Huygens, who postulated that light traveled in waves. It was no easy task to reach a conclusion, and scientists argued this issue for 100 years. As scientists studied both light and matter at atomic and subatomic levels, they developed what came to be known as quantum mechanics, which helped demonstrate that both light and matter have some characteristics of particles and some characteristics of waves.

Although relativity and quantum mechanics have dominated modern physics, the fundamentals of mechanics, heat, electricity, light, and other branches of physics are also crucial to our comprehension of the world around us. A single theory that encompasses all physical phenomena has yet to be discovered; however, physicists have made some astounding breakthroughs over the years.

The principles of Newtonian mechanics are evident almost everywhere. The action of kicking a ball, for instance, exemplifies Newton's second law of motion. Shutterstock.com

CHAPTER 1

THE SCOPE OF PHYSICS

Without the science of physics and the work of physicists, our modern ways of living would not exist. Instead of having brilliant, steady electric light, we would have to read by the light of candles, oil lamps, or at best, flickering gaslight. We might have buildings several stories high, but there could be no hope of erecting an Empire State Building. We could not possibly bridge the Hudson River or the Golden Gate much less build a jet plane, use a cell phone, or watch a television show. The personal computer would be unimaginable.

A FUNDAMENTAL SCIENCE

There is no exact distinction between physics and other natural sciences because all sciences overlap. In general, however, physics deals with phenomena that pertain to all

Statics figures prominently in the design and construction of structures such as the Golden Gate Bridge. Shutterstock.com

classes of matter and energy. Physicists try to discover the most basic laws of nature, which underlie and often explain those of other fields of science.

All other natural sciences depend upon physics for the foundations of their knowledge. For example, modern physics has discovered how atoms are made up of smaller particles. It has also revealed how these

particles interact to join atoms into molecules and larger masses of matter. Chemists use this knowledge to guide them in their work in studying all existing chemical compounds and in making new ones.

Biologists and medical researchers in turn use both physics and chemistry in studying living tissues and in developing new drugs and treatments. Furthermore the electrical equipment, microscopes, and X-rays and the use of radioactivity on which they depend were developed originally by physicists.

BRANCHES OF PHYSICS

One major branch of physics, mechanics, deals with the states of matter—solids, liquids, and gases—and their motions. The pioneer achievements of the scientists Galileo, Johannes Kepler, and Isaac Newton dealt with solid masses of matter in motion. Such studies are a part of the subdivision of mechanics called dynamics, the study of matter in motion.

The other great subdivision of mechanics is statics, the study of matter at rest. Statics deals with the balancing of forces and resistances to keep matter at rest. The design of buildings and of bridges are examples of problems in statics.

Other divisions of physics are based on the different kinds of energy that interact with matter. They deal with electricity and magnetism, heat, light, and sound. The study of the

Even something as ordinary as a shaft of light illustrates numerous physical concepts. The branch of physics dedicated to the study of light is called optics. Shutterstock.com

behavior of light is called optics, and that of sound is called acoustics. Thermodynamics is the study of the relationship between heat, work, temperature, and energy. From these branches of physics have come clues that have revealed how atoms are constructed and how they react to various kinds of energy. This knowledge is often called the basis of modern physics. Among the many subdivisions of modern physics are electronics and nuclear physics.

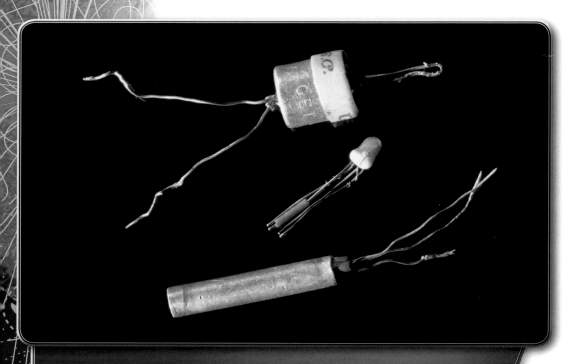

Early British transistors. **SSPL via Getty Images**

THE SCIENTIFIC REVOLUTION

Physicists have been instrumental in getting people to think in scientific ways. What we call the scientific method had its real beginnings some four centuries ago in many fields of knowledge. The most impressive of the early triumphs came in physics and in its application to astronomy for studying the motions of the Sun, Moon, planets, and stars.

An illustration of Newton's reflecting telescope. **Dorling Kindersley/the Agency Collection/ Getty Images**

Galileo made the first real contributions, in the late 16th and early 17th century. He discovered the natural laws that govern falling objects and the swinging of the pendulum (a weight suspended from a wire so that it can swing back and forth under the influence of gravity). Shortly after this, Johannes Kepler established the three laws that explain all the motions of the planets. Finally, in the late 17th century Isaac Newton explained these results by establishing the law of gravitation. This law applies invariably to all matter in the universe—whether as small as a grain of sand or as large as the Sun. This triumph of explaining a vast range of phenomena with a single law inspired workers in all fields of knowledge to trust scientific methods.

This revolution in understanding was greatly aided by advances in technology. Instruments such as clocks, barometers (which measure the pressure of the atmosphere), and telescopes were invented and improved. For example, Galileo, Kepler, and Newton made contributions to the development of telescopes and thus gave astronomy a powerful instrument with which to work.

Computers, spacecraft, and telephones all owe their existence to condensed-matter physics. This branch of physics is concerned with the internal structure and properties of solids and liquids. Among its many triumphs in the 20th century was the development of the transistor, a basic component of modern electronics equipment.

Nuclear physicists study the structure of the nucleus, the dense core of the atom. They also study the special forces that act between nuclear particles, the radiation from unstable nuclei, and nuclear reactions. The energy released during nuclear reactions has been put to use in nuclear power plants and in nuclear weapons.

Particle, or high-energy, physics is closely related to nuclear physics. It is the study of the most fundamental particles of which matter is made.

CHAPTER 2

SCIENTIFIC METHODS USED IN PHYSICS

Physics attempts to describe and explain the physical universe. Physicists therefore try to discover laws—invariable principles of nature at work—that will explain a large class of phenomena. Newton's law of gravitation is a prominent example, but there are many others as well.

THE LAWS OF PHYSICS

Physicists express these laws in mathematical form, which can serve later as a basis for measurements and calculations. For example, Newton's law of gravitation states that the force of gravitational attraction (F) between two separate objects depends on the amount of mass (m) of each one and the distance (R) between them. The masses must be multiplied together, and the pull diminishes according to the square of the distance. If the distance is doubled, for example, the gravitational pull is only one-fourth as great. The whole law can be stated in a short formula: $F = G(m_1 m_2)/R^2$, where G is the universal gravitational constant.

The law of gravitation has helped scientists plan the paths of spacecraft, such as the space shuttle **Endeavour. NASA**

This formula can be used in turn to give answers to a host of problems. Newton used it to help explain Kepler's laws. Later it was used to find the masses of other planets, stars, and galaxies. Today it is also used (with some corrections courtesy of Albert Einstein) to plan the paths of spacecraft.

HOW KNOWLEDGE OF PHYSICS DEVELOPED

Many ancient cultures demonstrated curiosity about the world around them. Through patient observation, they found patterns in nature that could be used to make certain kinds of predictions. For example, the ancient Egyptians noticed that when the star Sirius began rising in the morning before the Sun, the Nile River would soon flood. This prediction was of great practical importance because this flooding was the basis for their agriculture. However, without the tools and methods of physics, they had difficulty finding explanations for such patterns and were often content with the practical results they had obtained.

The ancient Greeks, however, were generally discontented with only simple

TESTING THE LAWS

Robert Millikan. **Apic/Hulton Archive/Getty Images**

Whenever possible, physicists try to discover laws and test them by experiments in which the variables involved can be controlled or measured accurately. For example, the American physicist Robert A. Millikan determined the fundamental unit of electricity, the charge carried by one electron (a negatively charged particle). He did so by making thousands of measurements upon microscopic droplets of oil that were kept dancing in a vacuum between oppositely charged metal plates.

Both conducting experiments and formulating theories play essential roles in the advancement of physics. Physical experiments result in measurements. Scientists compare these measurements with the outcome predicted by theory. A theory that reliably predicts the results of experiments is said to embody a law of physics. However, a law may need to be changed, limited, or replaced if a later experiment makes it necessary.

knowledge gained through practical experience and sought deeper explanations. They thought the world to be a rational place, with its "secrets" accessible to the powers of human intellect. This belief, along with the lack of good experimental methods, led many to try to explain nature through reason alone.

Naturally, different thinkers arrived at different opinions, and they argued passionately for them, often on the basis of such principles as beauty, symmetry, and simplicity. While experience has since shown such concepts to be indeed useful in physics, ancient thinkers had no objective way of determining who was right. Some propositions, such as Democritus' theory that matter is composed of elementary "atoms," turned out to be basically correct. Often, though, the theories were later overthrown. (For example, Ptolemy's theory that Earth was the center of the universe later had to be abandoned.) Nature had simply not yet been described accurately enough, or in sufficient detail, to make these attempted explanations meaningful.

Scientists began making progress almost two thousand years later, in Galileo's time,

Bronze bust of Democritus. Leemage/Universal Images Group/ Collection Mix: Subjects/Getty Images

by attacking specific problems that could be tested with well-defined methods. They let the formulation of more general theories wait until enough phenomena had been described in sufficient detail to warrant an explanation.

During the two centuries after Galileo's time, tremendous progress was made. By the early 1800s, physicists had won considerable basic knowledge about the interactions of specific forms of energy, such as heat, and matter. Even then, however, each type of interaction had to be studied separately. More than a century passed before anybody could begin to gather the interactions together into a general theory of the physical universe.

CHAPTER 3

MECHANICS

A survey of physics can best be made by proceeding as the physicists did, considering first the separate, specific types of interaction between matter and energy. The most basic topic in the study of physics is mechanics, which concerns the motion of objects being acted upon by forces. It establishes fundamental measurements that enter into all interactions. Different units are needed for measuring various forms of energy, such as light and electricity. However, physicists keep these units consistent with those used in mechanics. This practice helps to hold all the branches of physics together as one body of knowledge.

ANCIENT BEGINNINGS

Primitive humans maintained their place in the world by learning to use stone tools, bows and arrows, and other mechanical devices. No one knows when they began to use sticks as levers or how and when they developed the wheel, but it is known that the physics of simple machines and the science of measurement developed early.

In about 2600 BCE the Great Pyramid of Egypt was built with sides of very nearly the

Although the study of physics had not yet been formalized, the ancient Egyptians were able to construct the Great Pyramid and the other pyramids of Giza with great precision because of their grasp of certain basic concepts of mechanics. **Shanna Baker/ Flickr/Getty Images**

same length and corners that are very nearly right angles. This achievement required excellent measuring equipment and skill in using it.

In about 330 BCE the Greek philosopher and scientist Aristotle wrote the treatise *Physics*. This work was the dominant authority on the subject for many centuries. Although many principles contained in this work have proved valid, some are wrong. Perhaps the most famous is the statement that heavier objects fall through a given distance in less time than lighter ones; it was almost 2,000 years later before Galileo's experiments proved this to be incorrect.

Another great scientist of ancient Greece was Archimedes. One of his most famous discoveries was the law of buoyancy, which explains why objects float or sink in fluids. He also made important contributions to knowledge of levers and pulleys.

GALILEO FOUNDS MODERN MECHANICS

Although a number of important discoveries in mechanics were made in the 18 centuries between Aristotle and Galileo, it was the

Galileo. SSPL via Getty Images

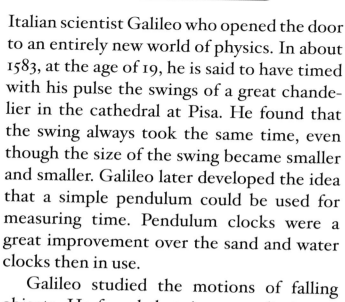

Italian scientist Galileo who opened the door to an entirely new world of physics. In about 1583, at the age of 19, he is said to have timed with his pulse the swings of a great chandelier in the cathedral at Pisa. He found that the swing always took the same time, even though the size of the swing became smaller and smaller. Galileo later developed the idea that a simple pendulum could be used for measuring time. Pendulum clocks were a great improvement over the sand and water clocks then in use.

Galileo studied the motions of falling objects. He found that, in contradiction to Aristotle's claim, heavy objects fall at exactly the same speeds as lighter ones when air friction is discounted. (Friction is a force that slows movement between objects that are rubbing against one another, such as air molecules and a falling ball.) Galileo also studied accelerated motion by rolling balls down inclined planes. His experiments laid the foundation for modern mechanics.

Some earlier scientists also had insisted upon careful observation and experiment as the way to win knowledge, rather than depending upon mere appearances. An example is Roger Bacon, an English philosopher, scientist, and friar who lived during the 13th

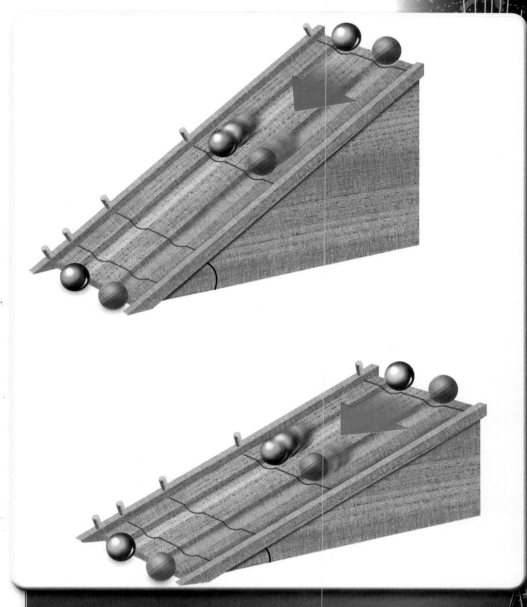

Illustrations of Galileo's experiments with accelerated motion down inclines of various gradients. **Dorling Kindersley/Getty Images**

century. Nonetheless Galileo is considered the father of the experimental, or scientific, method. He devised critical experiments that forced conviction even though the results contradicted earlier authorities.

NEWTON'S MONUMENTAL CONTRIBUTIONS

The same year Galileo died (1642), one of the greatest scientists of all time was born in England: Isaac Newton. His experiments with light laid the foundation for the modern science of optics. He also built the world's first reflecting telescope (a type that uses mirrors to focus light). His studies of falling objects and of the solar system led to his celebrated law of universal gravitation.

Newton concluded that an invisible force—gravity—acts between the Sun and its planets. He formulated a comparatively simple mathematical expression for the gravitational force (which was discussed in chapter 2). It states that every object in the universe attracts every other object with a force that operates through empty space. This force varies with the masses of the objects and the distance between them.

From his experiments with light and optics to his formulation of the law of gravitation, Isaac Newton had a critical impact on the field of physics. **Hulton Archive/Getty Images**

Newton discovered many of the basic laws of mechanics, including the fundamental laws of motion. He also developed a special mathematics for treating problems in mechanics. Thus he became one of the discoverers of the branch of mathematics known as calculus. He provided firm bases for expressing natural laws as mathematical formulas.

Newton took as a working principle that objects remain motionless or in uniform motion (constant speed in a straight line) unless something happens to produce a change. Newton called this something a force, and he provided methods for measuring mechanical forces.

NEWTON'S LAWS OF MOTION

Newton published his three laws of motion in 1687. These laws describe the relations between the forces (pushes or pulls) acting on an object and the motion of the object.

The first law states that, if an object is at rest (not moving), it will remain at rest unless a force acts upon it. Likewise, if an object is moving in a straight line at a constant speed, it will keep moving in a straight line at that speed unless a force causes it to change its direction or its speed, or both. This principle

According to Newton's third law, a ball that is hit with a tennis racket will exert a force on the racket that is equal in magnitude and opposite in direction to that of the force exerted on the ball.
Ted Stewart Photography/Stone/Getty Images

THE SUCCESS OF NEWTONIAN MECHANICS

Scientific reasoning based upon Newton's laws came to be called Newtonian mechanics. In the 20th century it also became known as classical physics. Newtonian mechanics was remarkably successful in accounting for the motions of the Moon, Earth, and other planets. In fact, Newton's methods adequately explained all known motions and mechanical effects for some two centuries after his time.

During the 18th and 19th centuries many scientists developed Newtonian mechanics into a well-integrated and mature science. Among them were Leonhard Euler, members of the Bernoulli family, Joseph-Louis Lagrange, Jean Le Rond d'Alembert, and Gustave-Gaspard Coriolis. They applied Newton's laws to ever more complex combinations of forces and motions in three dimensions.

had been discovered by Galileo and perfected by the French scientist and philosopher René Descartes.

Newton's second law is one of the most important laws in all of physics. It concerns the changes that a force can produce on an object's motion. A force can change an object's speed, the direction of its motion, or both. An object's velocity expresses both how fast and in what direction the object is moving. Acceleration is the rate at which an object's velocity changes.

According to Newton's second law, when a force acts on an object, it produces a change in the velocity of the object in the direction of the force. The magnitude (size or strength) of the acceleration is proportional to the magnitude of the force. For example, if a person kicks a ball, the ball will move in the direction it was kicked. The stronger the kick and the lighter (less massive) the ball, the greater the acceleration. The force (F) acting on an object is equal to the mass (m) of the object times its acceleration (a), or $F = ma$.

Newton's third law states that when two objects interact, they apply forces to one another that are equal in strength and opposite in direction. In other words, for every action (or force), there is an equal and opposite reaction (force). When a person hits a ball with a tennis racket, the force of the racket causes the ball to experience a sudden change in motion. At the same time, the ball exerts an equal and opposite force on the racket. This force pushes backward on the racket, and the player feels the shock of the impact.

CHAPTER 4

RELATIVITY

B y the late 19th century, Newtonian mechanics had triumphed in so many areas that some physicists began to believe that physics itself was nearly complete. Such speculations soon proved premature. In 1873 the Scottish physicist James Clerk Maxwell showed that light travels as a wave. This remarkable finding raised an important question: if light is a moving wave, what substance supports it? Ocean waves consist of the vibrations (tiny back-and-forth movements) of molecules of water. Sound waves are formed of the vibrations of molecules of gases in the air. But what vibrates to make a moving light wave? Or to put it another way, how does the energy embodied in light travel from point to point?

Scientists of the time believed that light traveled through an invisible substance called the ether. Supposedly, this ether was spread through all of space but did not interfere with

James Clerk Maxwell. Hulton Archive/Getty Images

the motion of the planets and stars. Scientists thought that Earth moved ("drifted") through the ether. In 1887 the American physicists A.A. Michelson and E.W. Morley tried to measure this drift. Although they made extremely precise measurements, they detected no sign of Earth's motion. This surprising result meant that there was no such thing as ether. It also showed that Newtonian mechanics could not explain the behavior of light.

Michelson and Morley had measured the speed of light accurately as it traveled both in the same direction as Earth's movement and in the direction opposite to Earth's movement. They expected to get slightly different values. They believed that Earth's speed would be added to or subtracted from the speed of light. This is similar to a situation in which a passenger in a train moving at 100 miles per hour shoots an arrow in the train's direction of motion at 200 miles per hour. An observer standing by the tracks would measure the speed of the arrow as the sum of the two speeds, or 300 miles per hour.

Michelson and Morley discovered, however, that light does not behave that way. The speed of light is about 186,300 miles (299,800 kilometers) per second. Evidently, the speed

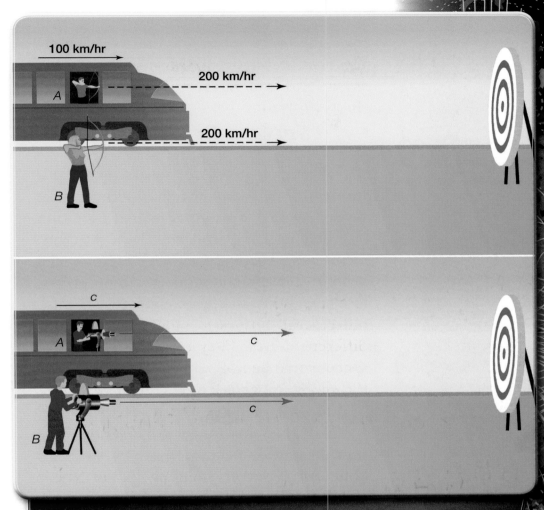

Arrows shot from a moving train (A) and from a stationary loca-tion (B) will arrive at a target at different velocities—in this case, 300 and 200 kilometers per hour (km/hr), respectively, because of the motion of the train. However, such commonsense addition of velocities does not apply to light. Even for a train traveling at the speed of light, both laser beams, A and B, have the same velocity: c.
Encyclopædia Britannica, Inc.

of light plus any other added speed was still equal only to the speed of light. To explain the result of the Michelson-Morley experiment, physics had to be recast on a new foundation.

SPECIAL RELATIVITY

Physicists struggled for years with this problem. Finally, in 1905 the German-born physicist Albert Einstein provided a solution with his first, or special, theory of relativity. He took as a working principle that the speed of light is always the same for all observers, no matter how fast they are moving. He also said that all observers moving at constant speeds in a straight line should be able to discover the same laws of physics, whether in the realm of mechanics, or of electricity, magnetism, and light.

Through mathematical equations, Einstein showed that, if these two principles were true, Newton's concepts of space and time could not be correct. In Newtonian mechanics, space and time are "absolute." In other words, it is assumed that all observers everywhere in the universe will obtain identical measurements of space and time. According to special relativity, observers in motion relative to one another will not obtain the same measurements of space and time. Einstein also considered space and time to be aspects of a single entity, called "space-time." He further determined that light travels at the fastest possible speed in the universe; material objects can approach but never reach its speed.

Special relativity draws many startling conclusions

Albert Einstein. Library of Congress Prints and Photographs Division

that are contrary to everyday experience. For instance, it concludes that as a body moves faster, it becomes smaller along its direction of motion. Time also runs more slowly for the body than it does for something that is not moving as fast. At the speeds of everyday life, these differences are so tiny as to be unnoticeable. (At lower speeds, the predictions of relativity thus match Newton's beautifully.) At extremely large speeds, the differences in measurements are much greater. For example,

$E = MC^2$

A nuclear missile. Michael Dunning/ Photographer's Choice/Getty Images

From the theory of special relativity Einstein derived perhaps the most famous equation in all of science: $E = mc^2$. Scientists had long believed that matter and energy were two different things. This elegant equation overturned that idea. It expresses the fact that mass and energy are the same physical entity. In the equation, E stands for energy, m for mass, and c for the speed of light (which is a constant). Energy can thus be changed into mass, and mass can be changed into energy.

The equation $E = mc^2$ is essential in the study of subatomic particles (particles smaller than atoms). Because the speed of light squared is such a large value, the equation shows that a small quantity of matter is the equivalent of an enormous quantity of energy. Nuclear bombs and nuclear power plants are designed to make use of this fact. In one type of nuclear reaction, the heavy nucleus of an atom is split into two lighter nuclei. Afterward, the total mass of the two nuclei is slightly less than what had been the mass of the heavy nucleus before the reaction. The tiny amount of "missing" mass was converted into a huge amount of energy.

suppose that one of two identical twins flies off to a distant star at nearly the speed of light. When she returns to Earth she finds that she is much younger than the twin she had left behind. Because the first twin had been traveling in a spacecraft at an extremely fast speed, time passed more slowly for her. As strange as such results are, numerous experiments have shown special relativity to be true.

GENERAL RELATIVITY

In 1916 Einstein published his second, or general, theory of relativity, which concerns gravity. As in special relativity, the predictions match those of Newton quite closely in ordinary circumstances. However, the predictions depart significantly when the values involved are very great—in this case when gravity is especially strong.

Whereas Newton thought that gravity was a force, Einstein showed that gravity arises from the shape of space-time. Each mass in the universe bends the very structure of space-time around it. This concept is difficult to visualize, but an analogy can provide some insight. Consider space-time to be a rubber sheet spread out flat. Imagine that a bowling ball (representing the Sun) is

placed on the sheet. The ball will curve the sheet (space-time) around it, creating a cup-like depression. Next, imagine that a marble is also put on the sheet. A smaller depression will form around the marble. If the marble is placed near the bowling ball's depression, it will roll down the slope toward the ball as if pulled by a force. If the marble is given a side-ways push, it will travel around the bowling ball like a planet orbits the Sun. It is as if a steady pull toward the ball swings the marble into a closed path.

Both of Einstein's relativity theories have so far proved correct in every case in which it has been possible to test them. Today rela-tivistic corrections to Newtonian mechanics are made whenever needed. These theories, together with other 20th-century devel-opments, have been particularly helpful in working out the modern theory of the atom. They are also the basis for models of the entire universe.

CHAPTER 5

HEAT

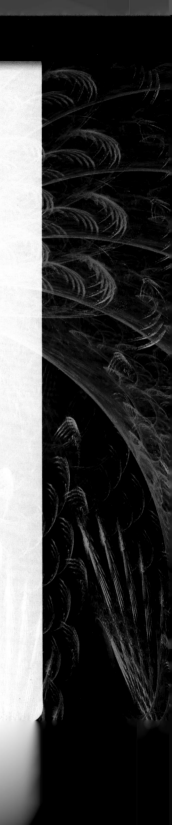

Physicists now regard heat as being essentially the energy of motion of the tiny molecules that make up most matter. This theory, called the kinetic molecular theory, was developed largely in the 19th century. It was not established, however, until after centuries of working with mistaken concepts.

OLD AND NEW CONCEPTS OF HEAT

The ancients thought that heat was an element. It therefore could be analyzed only as a physical entity that flows into and out of substances. This idea endured for centuries. Even as brilliant a scientist as Antoine-Laurent Lavoisier, a French chemist of the late 18th century, considered heat as a fluid of some sort. He called this fluid caloric.

Experiments constantly disproved this view. Weighing matter when it was hot, then cold, showed no change that would correspond to a flow of caloric in or out of the substance. In the late 18th and early 19th century a group of physicists, including Benjamin Thompson of Great Britain, developed a new theory of heat. They reasoned that motion is transformed into heat (as when a bullet strikes through a piece of wood). Thus they concluded that heat is not an element or a substance. It is a result rather of the constant motion of the invisible particles that compose matter, which we now call molecules. Many different experiments confirmed this and thus established the kinetic molecular theory.

This theory proved satisfactory for explaining the heat energy contained in matter. At the same time physicists developed another theory to explain radiant heat, or heat transmitted through radiation such as light, rather than through matter. They concluded that radiant heat passing through empty space in the form of light is a type of wave. The waves are emitted by a hot body such as the Sun. When they strike matter (as on Earth), they stimulate the molecules in

Benjamin Thompson. Apic/Hulton Archive/Getty Images

HEAT AND TEMPERATURE

If a hot poker is plunged into cold water, the poker becomes cooler and the water becomes warmer. The energy transferred from one object to another because of a difference in temperature is known as heat. Heat results from the constant, random motions of the individual molecules that make up matter. This energy of motion is known as kinetic energy. Temperature expresses how hot or cold something is. It is a measure of the average kinetic energy of an object's molecules, or how fast on average the molecules are moving.

Heat flows from a hotter object to a colder object when the two objects are brought together. This transfer of energy continues until the two objects have the same temperature. The transfer of heat between them will then stop. If a bowl of hot soup is left out on the counter, for example, the soup will gradually cool off as it transfers heat to the cooler air around it. Eventually, the soup is the same temperature as the air, and the heat transfer ceases.

As a bowl of hot soup cools, it transfers heat to the surrounding air until both the air and the soup are the same temperature. Shutterstock.com

the matter to greater motion. This "heats" the matter.

PLANCK'S QUANTUM THEORY OF HEAT

According to the kinetic molecular theory, heat can be emitted and absorbed in any amount. Heat thus can be divided into infinitely smaller amounts. In 1900, however, the German physicist Max Planck forced a change in this view.

Physicists had been experimenting with a device that absorbs essentially all the heat energy sent into it. The device then reradiates the energy as light of all different wavelengths, including infrared radiation, visible light, and ultraviolet radiation. If heat energy could indeed be divided into smaller and smaller amounts, the energy emitted in these experiments would have a particular distribution of wavelengths. But it did not. The energy emitted had far less radiation at shorter wavelengths than predicted.

Planck found a rather different—and quite successful—explanation for the observed distribution of wavelengths in these experiments. He proposed that radiant heat energy

49

Max Planck. **Hulton Archive/Getty Images**

is not infinitely divisible. Instead, it is transferred in exact amounts, more like particles than like waves. There is thus a certain smallest particle that cannot be divided. Planck called this smallest particle a quantum.

Because Planck's experiments were unquestionably accurate, physicists had to accept this quantum theory. Soon the same sort of indivisible unit was found in light and in electricity, and today the quantum theory ranks with relativity as one of the cornerstones of modern physics. The only change from Planck's view is a later theory that says that quanta travel in association with waves, which is discussed in chapter 7.

CHAPTER 6

LIGHT, ELECTRICITY, AND MAGNETISM

The ancients were familiar with many optical phenomena such as shadows, rainbows, and the use of fire in lamps to produce light. They knew about reflection and refraction (such as the bending of light when it goes from water to air). They also made and used lenses.

In 1608 a Dutch optician named Hans Lippershey built what may have been the first telescope. Shortly after, Galileo made a telescope and used it to discover Jupiter's major moons, sunspots, and the rotation of the Sun. At about this same time the microscope came into use. These optical instruments made possible great strides in astronomy and the biological sciences.

READING THE RIDDLES OF ELECTRICITY

Physicists eventually discovered that light is the result of electrical activity in atoms.

Reflection, refraction, and other optical occurrences are illustrated in rainbows and other natural phenomena. Shutterstock.com

Knowledge of electricity is thus necessary to understand the behavior and properties of light. Lightning, electric eels, and magnetic stones had been known since ancient times. The ancients also knew that if one rubbed a piece of amber with fur, it would attract bits of straw. Nevertheless, knowledge of

ACOUSTICS: THE SCIENCE OF SOUND

Much of what is known about the world was learned through sight and hearing. The ancients naturally were interested in light and sound. Of the two, sound was much easier to understand, and people began discovering facts about sound at an early date.

The physics of sound is called acoustics. Humans' love of music led them to build musical instruments from which they learned that all bodies that produce sounds are vibrating. Faster vibrations produce sound of higher pitch; and slower vibrations, lower pitch.

A guitar string produces sound based on the vibrations that are created when it is plucked. Shutterstock.com

The ancient Greek mathematician Pythagoras was the founder of acoustics. He investigated the laws of stringed instruments in the 6th century BCE. Some 500 years later Vitruvius, a Roman architectural engineer, wrote that sound is produced as a series of circular waves like those made by a stone when it is thrown into still water. Today, it is known that sound waves consist of an ever-widening sphere of compressions, regions where the air molecules are crowded together. These compressions are separated by regions where the molecules are farther apart than usual.

The first known attempts to measure the speed of sound came in the early 17th century. Later Newton developed a theory that predicts the speed of sound from the elastic properties of the air, according to Newtonian mechanical principles.

electricity developed much more slowly than any other branch of classical physics.

In the 17th and 18th centuries this previously neglected subject received much attention. It was shown that many materials could be "electrified" by rubbing them with silk or fur. Such experiments seemed to indicate that two kinds of electricity (called charges) might exist. Each seemed to repel others of the same kind and attract their opposites. This could happen only if there were two kinds of charges or if one kind existed in excess and deficiency—that is, in

Lightning is naturally occurring electrical discharge that is often visible during thunderstorms. Shutterstock.com

positive (+) and negative (–) amounts. The latter view turned out to be correct. An excess would tend to flow toward (be attracted by) a deficiency.

During this period, experimenters were hampered by the fact that whenever a path was formed between opposite charges, the charges seemed to unite almost instantly. Then in 1800 the Italian physicist Alessandro Volta announced his discovery of an electric battery that would produce a steady flow of direct electric current. This invention stimulated research in electricity to an unprecedented degree. The scientists Humphry Davy, Hans Christian Ørsted, and Michael Faraday used this new source of electricity to discover many new facts. They found, for example, that an electric current can be used to break up dissolved substances, in a process called electrolysis. They also discovered that an electric current can generate magnetism and vice versa.

THE ELECTROMAGNETIC SPECTRUM

Electric charges as well as current and magnetism exert influence across space. In 1873 James Clerk Maxwell published his highly significant theory of electromagnetism, which brought the phenomena of electricity, magnetism, and light together in a unified framework. He theorized that electromagnetism moves across space at the speed of light in waves composed of electric and magnetic

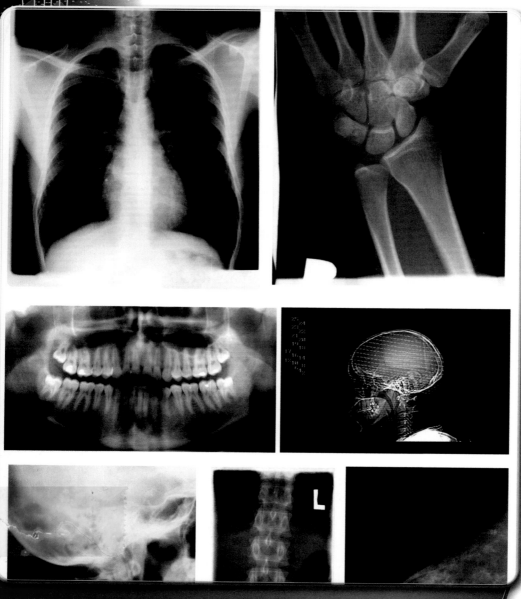

Wilhelm Roentgen's pioneering work with electromagnetic radiation led to his discovery of X-rays, which are used today to produce X-ray images such as these. Shutterstock.com

fields. He also concluded that light is such an electromagnetic wave.

In the 1880s the German physicist Heinrich Hertz deliberately produced and detected electromagnetic waves. The waves he produced had wavelengths far longer than those of visible light; they are now known as radio waves. The Italian physicist Guglielmo Marconi used this discovery in developing the radio.

Infrared and ultraviolet radiation were found to fit the electromagnetic wave model as well. So did X-rays, which were discovered by the German physicist Wilhelm Roentgen in 1895. The various forms of electromagnetic radiation known today include (from longest to shortest wavelengths) radio and television waves, microwaves, infrared radiation, visible light, ultraviolet radiation, X-rays, and gamma rays. Together they make up the electromagnetic spectrum.

CHAPTER 7

LIGHT: WAVE OR PARTICLE?

I n the mid-17th century two great physicists performed experiments with light and arrived at two quite different conclusions. Newton accepted the theory that light rays are streams of tiny particles. He believed that light bends as it goes from air to water because the particles are attracted toward and pulled downward into the water, gaining speed as they enter the water. The Dutch physicist Christiaan Huygens developed a wave theory of light. According to his wave theory, light bends when it goes from air to water because the waves move more slowly in water than in air.

THE PROBLEM OF EXPLAINING LIGHT

For more than 100 years the argument raged between supporters of the particle and wave theories. At length certain experiments gave support to the wave theory. When two beams of light overlap at a point, they may add to each other to produce brighter light. However, they may instead cancel one another out and produce darkness. This phenomenon is called interference, and it is a property of waves. Shortly after 1800, Thomas Young of England and later Augustin-Jean Fresnel of France performed many experiments that demonstrated the interference of light. Their results supported the wave theory.

In about 1850 the French physicists François Arago, Jean Foucault, and Armand-Hippolyte-Louis Fizeau showed that light travels faster in air than in water—just as Huygens had concluded. This was a great triumph for the wave theory, and it convinced physicists that it was the correct explanation.

The work of Maxwell and Hertz also seemed to prove that all electromagnetism, including light, moves in waves. But another phase of Hertz's work (and work done by others) revived the particle theory.

During his experiments, Hertz had found that light falling upon metal can drive out a negative charge. The wave theory is unable to account for this phenomenon, which is

Christiaan Huygens. **Hulton Archive/Getty Images**

called the photoelectric effect. This effect can be explained only if light consists of particles. Einstein solved this problem in 1905. He proposed that light interacts with the surface of the metal as a particle (called a photon). However, the energy of the particle is directly proportional to the frequency of the light's wavelike vibrations—which is what Planck had assumed when developing his quantum theory. It turns out that, in some sense, Newton and Huygens were both right.

THE NATURE OF ELECTRICITY AND THE ATOM

It is now known that the negative charge knocked out of metal by the photoelectric effect consists of electrons. In 1897 the English physicist J.J. Thomson proved that electrons exist and that they are one of the building blocks of atoms. It thus became clear that atoms are made of smaller electrified particles. It also became clear that free electrons exert a negative charge. Scientists discovered that electric current consists of electrons moving through a material that acts as a conductor. Thus electricity and atoms are intimately connected, and both are particle in nature.

Because atoms are electrically neutral, scientists realized that they must contain positive and negative charges in equal amounts. The negative charge is in the form of electrons. In 1911 the British physicist Ernest Rutherford concluded from experiments that the positive charge is contained in a tiny

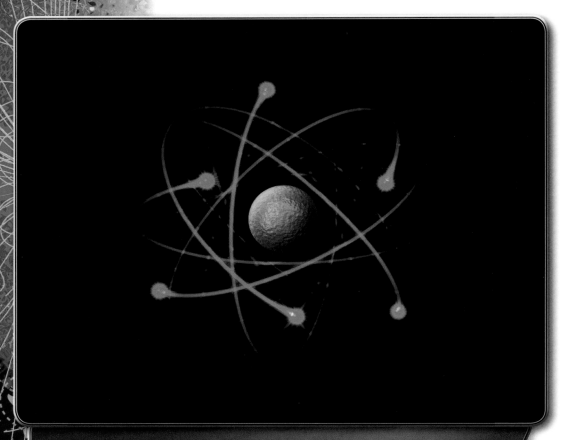

The Rutherford model of the atom, with electrons orbiting a nucleus. **Dorling Kindersley/the Agency Collection/Getty Images**

nucleus, with most of the atom being empty space. He thought that the electron might orbit the nucleus, much like a planet orbits the Sun.

THE BIRTH OF QUANTUM MECHANICS

In 1913 the Danish physicist Niels Bohr developed a model of the atom based on Planck's quantum theory. Bohr's model explained how the negatively charged electrons and the positively charged nucleus could coexist in an atom. He theorized that only certain, specific amounts of orbital energy are possible in an atom and that this allows it to exist in stable states. If the electron in an atom suddenly "falls" from a higher energy to a lower one, it gives off an exact amount of energy in the form of a photon of light, whose wavelength is determined from its energy.

Light, which had seemed earlier to be a wave, now seemed to have definite particle properties. In 1923 the French physicist Louis de Broglie suggested that particles such as electrons also might travel in the form of waves. This was confirmed in 1927 by Clinton Davisson and Lester Germer. Thus it seemed that both the particle theory and the wave

Niels Bohr. **Keystone/Hulton Archive/Getty Images**

theory must be correct, for both light and matter. The problem was to find how both could be true.

By 1927 physicists accomplished this by developing a consistent body of physical laws called quantum mechanics. Quantum mechanics is an outgrowth of Planck's quantum theory. It is the branch of physics that deals with the behavior of matter and light at atomic and subatomic scales. Among the founders of quantum mechanics were the mathematical physicists Max Born, Werner Heisenberg, de Broglie, Erwin Schrödinger, P.A.M. Dirac, and Pascual Jordan.

Heisenberg stated that it is impossible to measure, simultaneously and exactly, both the position and the velocity of a particle. The more accurately one measures the position, the less accurately one can measure the velocity, and vice versa. Schrödinger developed an equation that describes the wave that governs the motion of the associated particle. According to this equation, the particle is most likely to be found in those places where the undulations of the wave are greatest or most intense. Schrödinger's wave equation became the fundamental equation of quantum mechanics. The theory does not

RANDOMNESS AND PROBABILITY

One of the great ideas of the 20th century, quantum mechanics continues to be at the forefront of advances in physics in the 21st century. In addition to explaining the structure of atoms and the

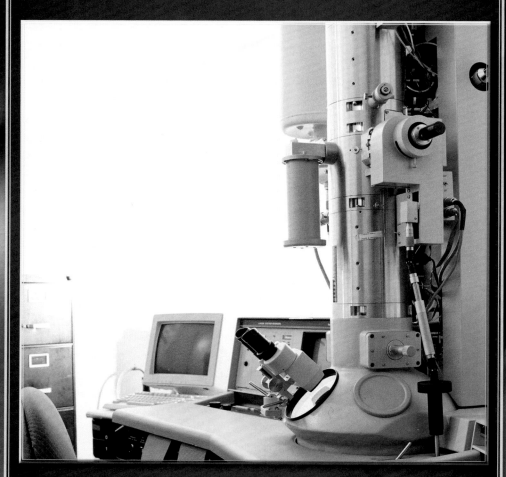

An electron microscope, one of the many products whose invention was enabled by the development of quantum mechanics. **Stephen Schauer/The Image Bank/Getty Images**

behavior of subatomic particles, it has explained the nature of chemical bonds, nuclear energy, and the forces that stabilize collapsed stars. Quantum theory also led directly to the invention of the laser, the electron microscope, and the transistor.

Quantum mechanics has revealed that matter and radiation behave much differently at extremely small scales than at the larger, familiar scales of the everyday world. At atomic scales the behavior of matter and radiation can seem unusual or downright bizarre. The concepts of quantum mechanics often conflict with common sense notions, notions that of course have been developed through observations of the world at larger scales. Niels Bohr famously said that "anybody who is not shocked by this subject has failed to understand it."

While the laws of Newtonian mechanics allow one to determine exactly how matter and radiation will behave, quantum mechanics deals only in probabilities. Indeterminacy — randomness or uncertainty — is fundamental to quantum mechanics. Nevertheless, the success of this field is indisputable. Using probabilities, quantum mechanics makes precise predictions about the properties of atomic and subatomic systems. In experiments these predictions have been shown to be extraordinarily accurate — more accurate in fact than those of any other branch of physics.

explain how the wave pattern arises or why it directs the movement of particles but simply describes in mathematical terms how the latter happens.

Conclusion

The ultimate aim of physics is to find a unified set of laws governing all matter, motion, and energy, large and small. In other words, physicists are trying to discover a single set of laws to explain all natural phenomena at the tiny distances of microscopic particles, at the human scale of everyday life, and at the largest distances of the universe.

A completely unified theory of physical phenomena has not yet been achieved—and possibly never will be. Nevertheless, physicists have realized this ambitious goal to a notable extent. A remarkably small set of fundamental physical laws appears able to account for all known phenomena. The body of physics developed up to about the start of the 20th century—called Newtonian mechanics or classical physics—can largely account for the motions of nonmicroscopic objects whose speeds do not approach the speed of light. It can also largely explain such phenomena as heat, sound, electricity, magnetism, and light. The modern developments of relativity and quantum mechanics are used to modify the laws of classical physics when necessary. Relativity applies to extremely high speeds or very massive objects, while quantum mechanics applies to the tiny elementary parts of matter, such as electrons, protons, and neutrons. Even as physicists continue to grapple with some of the greatest unknowns in the universe, they rely on the principles established by both classical and modern physics.

Glossary

acceleration Rate of change of velocity with respect to time.

acoustics Science of the production, control, transmission, reception, and effects of sound.

atom Smallest particle of matter that has the properties of a chemical element; can exist either alone or in combination.

caloric Supposed form of matter formerly thought to be responsible for the phenomena of heat and combustion.

condensed-matter physics Discipline that treats the thermal, elastic, electrical, magnetic, and optical properties of solid and liquid substances.

dynamics Branch of mechanics that deals with the motion of objects in relation to force, mass, momentum, and energy.

electric charge Quantity of electricity that flows in electric currents or that accumulates on the surfaces of dissimilar nonmetallic substances that are rubbed together briskly.

electrolysis Process in which electric current passed through a substance causes a chemical change, usually the gaining or losing of electrons.

electromagnetism Magnetism developed
by a current of electricity, or the b ranch
of physics that deals with the relationship between electricity and magnetism.

electron Negatively charged particle, the
lightest stable subatomic particle known.

electronics Branch of physics that deals
with the emission, behavior, and effects
of electrons (as in electron tubes and
transistors) and with electronic devices.

ether Theoretical substance believed by
19th-century scientists to permeate all of
space and to carry light waves.

force Agency that alters the direction,
speed, or shape that a body would exhibit
in the absence of any external influence.

interference Mutual effect on the meeting
of two wave trains (as of light or sound)
that constitutes alternating areas of
increased and decreased extent (as light
and dark lines or louder and softer sound).

law of gravitation Statement that any particle in the universe attracts any other
particle with a force that is proportional
to the product of the masses of the two
particles and inversely proportional to
the square of the distance between them.

magnetism Phenomenon associated with magnetic fields, the effects of such fields, and the motion of electric charges.

mass Quantitative measure of inertia (the resistance of a body to a change in motion).

mechanics Branch of physics that deals with the behavior of bodies under the influence of forces.

molecule Smallest unit into which a compound can be divided without changing its chemical properties.

nuclear physics Branch of physics dealing with the structure of the atomic nucleus and radiation from unstable nuclei.

optics Branch of physics concerned with the nature, properties, and behavior of light, including how it is produced and transmitted.

particle physics Study of the fundamental particles that make up matter.

photoelectric effect Phenomenon in which charged particles are released from a material when it absorbs radiant energy.

photon Extremely small packet of energy (or quantum) of electromagnetic radiation.

quantum Any of the extremely small units, or packets, into which many forms of energy are naturally subdivided.

quantum mechanics Branch of mathematical physics that deals with atomic and subatomic systems.

reflection Change in the direction of a wave as it strikes a boundary between different media through which it cannot pass (such as when light strikes a surface and bounces off).

refraction Change in the direction of a wave as it leaves one medium and enters another in which its speed is different (such as when light bends when traveling from air into water).

relativity Concept in physics that measurements change when considered by observers in various states of motion.

statics Branch of mechanics dealing with the balancing of forces that keeps bodies at rest.

transistor Electronic device used to control the flow of electricity in electronic equipment.

velocity Quantity that designates how fast and in what direction a point is moving.

wavelength Distance between corresponding points of two consecutive waves.

For More Information

American Institute of Physics (AIP)
One Physics Ellipse
College Park, MD 20740
(301) 209-3100
Web site: http://www.aip.org
The members of AIP consist of professionals, academics, and educators who seek to
promote the study of physics among the
public through programs, publications,
and outreach services.

Canadian Association of Physicists (CAP)
Suite 112, MacDonald Building
University of Ottawa
150 Louis Pasteur Priv.
Ottawa, ON K1N 6N5
Canada
(613) 562-5614
Web site: http://www.cap.ca
Committed to advancing research and edu-
cation in physics, CAP supports programs
for professionals pursuing physics-related
careers, sponsors lectures and competitions
for students, and provides information and
holds events for the public at large.

The Exploratorium
3601 Lyon Street
San Francisco, CA 94123

(415) 561-0360

Web site: http://www.exploratorium.edu

Through its extensive array of interactive exhibits and activities, the Exploratorium fosters curiosity about the the material world and excitement for all aspects of science and nature.

Science World at TELUS World of Science
1455 Quebec Street
Vancouver, BC V6A 3Z7
Canada
(604) 443-7443

Web site: http://www.scienceworld.ca

With interactive exhibits and educational programs in a variety of subject areas, including an extensive exhibit on electricity, Science World encourages the pursuit and enjoyment of scientific exploration among the public.

WEB SITES

Due to the changing nature of Internet links, Rosen Educational Services has developed an online list of Web sites related to the subject of this book. This site is updated regularly. Please use this link to access the list:

www.rosenlinks.com/inphy/sciph

Bibliography

Bonnet, R.L., et al. *Science Fair Projects: Physics* (Sterling, 2000). Cullen, K.E. *Physics: The People Behind the Science* (Chelsea House, 2006). Farndon, John. *Experimenting with Physics* (Benchmark, 2009). Fleisher, Paul. *Objects in Motion: Principles of Classical Mechanics* (Lerner, 2002). Fleisher, Paul. *Relativity and Quantum Mechanics: Principles of Modern Physics* (Lerner, 2002). Gallant, R.A. *The Ever Changing Atom* (Benchmark, 2000). Gilmore, Robert. *Alice in Quantumland: An Allegory of Quantum Physics* (Copernicus, 1995). Graham, John. *Forces and Motion* (Kingfisher, 2001). Green, Dan. *Physics: Why Matter Matters!* (Kingfisher, 2010). Hammond, Richard. *Can You Feel the Force?* (Dorling Kindersley, 2010). Stockley, Corrine, et al. *The Usborne Illustrated Dictionary of Physics* (Usborne, 2006).